MYSTERIOUS
DEATHS
AND
DISAPPEARANCES

Mysteries and Conspiracies™

MYSTERIOUS DEATHS AND DISAPPEARANCES

KOUTS
MS/HS
MEDIA CENTER

David Southwell and Sean Twist

ROSEN
PUBLISHING®

New York

North American edition first published in 2008 by:

The Rosen Publishing Group, Inc.
29 E. 21st Street
New York, NY 10010

North American edition copyright © 2008 by The Rosen Publishing Group, Inc. First published as *Conspiracy Theories* in Australia, copyright © 2004 by Carlton Books Limited. Text copyright © 2004 by David Southwell. Additional end matter copyright © The Rosen Publishing Group, Inc.

North American edition book design: Tahara Anderson

Library of Congress Cataloging-in-Publication

Southwell, David, 1971–
Mysterious deaths and disappearances / David Southwell and Sean Twist. — North American ed.
   p.cm. — (Mysteries and conspiracies)
ISBN-13: 978-1-4042-1081-3
ISBN-10: 1-4042-1081-4
1. Death — Miscellanea. 2. Conspiracies. 3. Celebrities — Death.
I. Twist, Sean. II. Title.
HQ1073.S68 2008
920.073–dc22

                                                          2007011990

Manufactured in the United States of America

On the cover: *(Right)* Chandra Levy; *(left)* Scene of David Kelly's death.

CONTENTS

1 AMELIA EARHART

She was the golden girl of the aviation set, a media celebrity, and an inspiration to women everywhere. Amelia Earhart strode into the male-dominated world of flying, setting new flight records for women, with a noble mix of courage and grace. Beloved by an America torn apart by the ravages of the Depression, Earhart was a national hero. Her sudden disappearance while trying to fly around the world in 1937 shocked the nation.

Amelia Earhart was born July 24, 1897, in Atchison, Kansas. Coming from a wealthy family, Earhart studied to be a nurse's aid in Toronto and worked as a Voluntary Aid Detachment nurse in a military hospital during World War I. In 1920, she moved to California with her family. It was there that she attended an aerial meet, and her love of flying was born. Quickly learning to fly, Earhart set a women's altitude

Amelia Earhart gets ready to take off from Newfoundland.

record of 14,000 feet (4,267 meters) two years later, and as the years passed, her reputation as a pilot flourished.

In 1928, New York publisher George Putnam asked her to become the first woman to cross the Atlantic on the "Friendship" flight between Great Britain and America. She agreed, setting yet another record. She was tagged with the name "Lady Lindy," after the first pilot to cross the Atlantic, Charles Lindbergh. Earhart disliked this name because she had merely been a passenger on the "Friendship" flight.

As if to prove herself even more, Earhart continued to set new records. In 1928, she flew across America, traveling from the Atlantic to the Pacific coast. In 1931, she set the altitude record of 14,000 feet in an autogiro. A year later, in 1932, Earhart flew across the Atlantic alone, landing in Ireland. She became the darling of the lecture tours and was honored by President Herbert Hoover and by Congress, becoming the first woman to receive the Distinguished Flying Cross. But her greatest challenge still lay before her—a flight around the world.

On June 1, 1937, Earhart flew out of Miami, Florida, in her Electra airplane to circumnavigate the globe. Accompanied only by her navigator, Fred Noonan, she set out first for Puerto Rico. From South America, they flew to Africa, then to the Red Sea. By June 29, they were in New Guinea, ready for the long flight across the Pacific. They were almost home. They left New Guinea at midnight on July 2, with the U.S. Coast Guard ship *Itasca* positioned off Howland Island, near Hawaii, to provide radio contact.

They never arrived at Howland Island. Earhart sent a message to the *Itasca* at 7:42 AM, saying that they were unable to see the ship and that their gas was running low. A brief message came through at 8:45 AM, then silence. The people of America, listening at their radios, were stunned. A shaken President Franklin Roosevelt sent out a military search party consisting of sixty-six aircraft and nine ships, but nothing was found. On July 18, 1937, the search was reluctantly called off. Amelia Earhart and Fred Noonan were gone.

THE STRANGE PART

In an uncharacteristic loss of control, Earhart made an error while trying to lift off from an airfield near Pearl Harbor. The undercarriage collapsed, severely damaging the plane. In what could be construed as an omen, it was the same plane she disappeared in over the Pacific.

THE USUAL SUSPECTS

Amelia Earhart

It was known that Earhart had suffered dysentery during the flight, perhaps impairing her judgement, causing her to crash.

It could also have been suicide—Earhart may have been burned out by the constant attention and expectations of the media. Or she could have simply chosen to disappear, setting up a new life after being away from the public eye. Some theories have her going to an isolated island to live peacefully with native fishermen.

The Nazi Party

It has been suggested that Earhart was on a secret mission for President Roosevelt to monitor Nazi activities around the globe. Shot down or captured by the Germans, this would explain the sizeable military force Roosevelt sent out to rescue her in an attempt, perhaps, to retrieve sensitive American information or useful data on the Nazis.

THE UNUSUAL SUSPECTS

Temporal Rift

Earhart may have flown into a temporal rift, which is what the Bermuda Triangle is rumored to be. This would explain the trouble with radio contact between the plane and *Itasca*, and her confusion. Perhaps her plane is simply lost in the past or the future.

The Japanese

Along the lines of the Nazi Party theory, this theory sees the Japanese capturing Earhart, coercing her to take to the airwaves as the dreaded "Tokyo Rose," the female propaganda machine that was a deadly scourge to GI morale during World War II.

The U.S. Government

If Earhart were an American spy, perhaps she discovered something disturbing about her employers. In retaliation, the U.S. Air Force would have shot down her plane, then valiantly mounted a search party for public relations purposes, while ensuring that no evidence remained.

Also suspected: UFOs; sea monsters.

MOST CONVINCING EVIDENCE

Despite the largest military search for civilians ever mounted, no wreckage or material from Earhart's plane was found at the time, suggesting that either Earhart was off course (with her formidable flying skills, this is doubtful), or the plane never crashed. None of the bones found since the disappearance have turned out to belong to her. Even recent evidence unearthed by the International Group for Historic Aircraft Recovery, suggesting her plane was at Gardner Island, failed to conclusively solve the mystery due to the absence of bones that proved a genetic match with Earhart.

MOST MYSTERIOUS FACT

For a week after Earhart's disappearance, several radio operators on ships and aircraft heard a distress signal coming from the vicinity of Gardner Island. It's possible Earhart may have landed there, but mysteriously nothing was ever found. Sixty years later, searchers believed they might have found items of Earhart's clothing, which rather begs the question: why wasn't this noticed before?

SKEPTICALLY SPEAKING

A light plane hitting the ocean at roughly 80 miles (128 kilometers) an hour would be like a car hitting a cement abutment at the same speed. Add scavengers like sharks and other hungry fish. End of mystery.

2 JIMMY HOFFA

The disappearance of Jimmy Hoffa has become the stuff of urban legend. The unknown whereabouts of the body of the ex-Teamsters union leader is a source of never-ending conjecture. What is even more compelling is that, while everyone is in agreement that Hoffa is indeed dead, no one has ever been arrested for killing him. The efforts of police, from Detroit detectives to the FBI, have not uncovered the killers. Their identities remain as mysterious as the final resting place of Hoffa himself.

James Riddle Hoffa was born February 14, 1913, in Brazil, Indiana. After getting a job as a warehouse employee at Kroger, a grocery store chain, Hoffa joined the International Brotherhood of Teamsters, a trade union. By 1957, Hoffa had climbed the union ladder to become president of the Teamsters, a position he held until 1971.

During his tenure as president of the Teamsters, Hoffa was often linked with the Mafia and with illegal activities.

Robert F. Kennedy investigated Hoffa in the 1950s and 1960s, which ended up with Hoffa being convicted for jury tampering (during an earlier trial in which Hoffa was accused of receiving illegal payments from a trucking firm). In 1967, Hoffa was sentenced to eight years in a federal prison. His sentence was commuted in 1970 by President Richard Nixon, with a condition of parole being that Hoffa should refrain from union activities until 1980.

This didn't impress Hoffa, who began to make moves to regain control of the Teamsters. By 1975, he was on the verge of success, but this didn't fit in with the future plans of the Mafia. Having had trouble with Hoffa, the Mafia hoped his successor, Frank Fitzsimmons, would prove more compliant. With the strong possibility that the stipulation barring Hoffa from union activities could be annulled, coupled with his strong loyalty base in the Teamsters, there was a chance that Hoffa could be president again. This was not something the Mafia wanted to see.

On Wednesday, July 30, 1975, Hoffa drove out to the Machus Red Fox Restaurant on Six Mile Road in Detroit, Michigan. It is known that he was due to meet someone there, but exactly who that was has never been revealed. Bearing in mind Hoffa's well-founded paranoia, it must have been someone he trusted. He was last seen alive at around 2:30 PM in the restaurant's parking lot. He then

Missing main man for the Mafia, Jimmy Hoffa

disappeared, surfacing again only in public myth and speculation.

THE STRANGE PART

The final resting place of Jimmy Hoffa remains a mystery, with claims ranging from the outrageous to the macabre. One story has him buried in the depths of Lake Michigan, while perhaps the most outrageous was the one put forth by Donald "Tony the Greek" Frankos, who told *Playboy* magazine that Hoffa was buried beneath the end zone of the New York Giants football stadium. More plausible theories have Hoffa's body placed in the foundations of a shopping mall, while the FBI is partial to the theory of Hoffa coming to rest in a vat of bubbling zinc in a Detroit car factory.

THE USUAL SUSPECTS

The Mafia

There was potential for the Mafia to make a lot of money from the Teamsters, especially with access to the massive Teamster pension funds. If an uncooperative Hoffa regained control of the Teamsters, the loss of this lucrative source of income would mean a sizeable financial setback to the Mafia. There were also rumors that Hoffa had told the government about the Mafia's involvement in the Teamsters as a condition of his restriction on union involvement being lifted. This alone would merit revenge in the eyes of the Mafia.

Tony Provenzano

Hoffa had upset some members of the Mafia on a more personal level, among them Tony Provenzano. "Tony Pro," as he was known, held a grudge against Hoffa from their time together in prison, and he may have put a contract out on the ex-Teamsters leader. He went to great pains to establish an alibi on the day of Hoffa's disappearance.

Chuckie O'Brien

Chuckie O'Brien may have been the man Hoffa expected to meet at the Red Fox, an apparently trustworthy decoy set up by the true killers. O'Brien grew up in Hoffa's home, effectively as an unofficial "adopted son," and he would not have been seen by Hoffa as a threat. O'Brien himself came under investigation when the police heard he was alleged to be in debt to the Mafia.

Union Officials

Not wanting to lose their positions within the union if Hoffa were elected president, some union officials may have put a contract out on him.

Also suspected: Tony Giacalone; Joseph Giacalone

THE UNUSUAL SUSPECTS

The Teamsters Union

Not wanting to experience the corrupt reign of Hoffa again, members of the Teamsters may have concluded that, in the light of his popularity with the membership, there was no other route to removing him than murder.

The FBI

A long-shot theory centers around the FBI. They may not have wanted the combative Hoffa to be in control of one of the most powerful unions in the United States, especially with Hoffa's grudge against law enforcement. Involvement in his disappearance would explain the bureau's "inability" to solve the case.

MOST CONVINCING EVIDENCE

The car Chuckie O'Brien was driving the day of Hoffa's disappearance was seized by the FBI. It was a new Mercury Brougham, belonging to Joseph Giacalone. Police dogs found Hoffa's scent in the back seat, as well as evidence of his blood and skin. O'Brien blamed the blood on a fish he was inexplicably delivering to a friend.

MOST MYSTERIOUS FACT

Knowing full well how the Mafia worked, Hoffa would never have gotten into a car with people he didn't trust—not without putting up a fight, at least. There's a darker element of betrayal to the story: whoever killed Hoffa, or led him to be killed, were friends he trusted to be loyal.

SKEPTICALLY SPEAKING

If you run with wolves, chances are you'll get bitten. The only thing that separates this from any other Mafia hit is the surprising lack of evidence buttressed by the silence of the killers. If Hoffa's body had been found, this would be nothing more than a half-forgotten footnote in the bloody history of Mafia business. As Mafia conspiracies go, it should be considered small-time—despite the way some conspiracy buffs view the case.

3 MARTIN LUTHER KING JR.

He was a man of peace, and like most men who try to make the world a better place, his life ended violently. Dr. Martin Luther King Jr. was an eloquent speaker, making moving speeches for civil rights in the 1960s, from the famous civil rights march of 200,000 people on Washington in 1963 to the more private confines of a church. He fought with dignity for a seemingly impossible goal—equal rights for all men and women, despite the color of their skin. During the turbulent sixties, many in America hoped King's dream would never come true.

King fought against bigotry and ignorance with weapons his enemies didn't expect: intelligence and compassion. He refused to stand down from what he believed in, angering those who felt blacks were nothing more than second-class citizens and should not dream of being anything more. King's quiet persistence raised fears of a changed status quo, from the Ku Klux Klan up to the FBI. He made powerful enemies and, in the end, they defeated him the only way they could, by silencing him forever.

Returning to Memphis in April 1968, King booked a room at the Motel Lorraine. He had returned to hold another demonstration, disgusted that an earlier protest held in the city in March had collapsed into violence. He was determined that this protest would not follow the same route. During his previous stay in Memphis, he had been criticized for staying in a white-owned hotel. To prove a point, King stayed in the Motel Lorraine, which was owned by blacks but was in a worse area of town.

On April 4, 1968, as evening was setting over Memphis, King was shot as he stood on the second-floor balcony of the Motel Lorraine. The threat to the status quo was eliminated. James Earl Ray, a local criminal, was arrested for the murder and was accused of shooting King from the bathroom of a nearby boarding house. Doubts, though, began to arise as to whether or not Ray was the true assassin.

THE STRANGE PART

James Earl Ray, who apparently had little money, somehow managed to become a world traveler following King's assassination. With his newfound wealth, he flew to Canada,

England, and then Portugal. When he was arrested in London's Heathrow Airport he was preparing to fly to Belgium.

THE USUAL SUSPECTS

The FBI

It was no secret that the head of the FBI, J. Edgar Hoover, thought King was one of the most dangerous men in America. In its attempts to remove King from his position of power, the FBI secretly taped King's alleged extramarital activities and used the tapes in the hope of convincing King to avoid public embarrassment by committing suicide. When that failed to work, there was only one alternative—the CIA.

Another theory suggests that King's assassins were provided by the CIA, disguised as Memphis police. Ray was framed for the crime; government agents carried out the actual killing. This would seem to be substantiated by the fact that when Ray was arrested, he was carrying several pieces of fake ID and more than one passport—documents rumored to be the work of a CIA identities specialist.

The Ku Klux Klan

King represented everything that the Klan hates. He was a man who refuted their stereotypes of blacks and threatened their narrow view of the world. By killing King, especially in the American South, the Klan would send a message to the black community graphically illustrating what happens to blacks who rise above their Klan-appointed station in life.

THE UNUSUAL SUSPECTS

The Memphis Police

Memphis was not particularly friendly to King, and the violent end to the demonstration in March 1968 did not endear him to the city, let alone to the police force. It has been rumored that CIA agents posed as policemen and killed King, but they may not have had to. The police could have had their own grudge against the civil rights leader, racially motivated or otherwise. It's interesting to note that the office of the director of the Memphis police force was heavily populated by members of the military shortly before the killing.

Inside Members of King's Party

It has been suggested that the conspiracy to kill King extended into his own camp. Rumors have persisted that more than one of his close followers was a spy for the police or FBI and may have helped throw pursuers off the scent of the true killers by pointing to the boarding house window after King was shot.

The Mob

The Mafia was allegedly approached by the FBI to kill King and offered a million dollars to do the job. The Mob refused, mysteriously citing the "screwups" the FBI caused directly after the assassination of John F. Kennedy, but they may have had second thoughts if the plot was sweetened.

MOST CONVINCING EVIDENCE

It is not just the conspiracy community that believes Ray was innocent. Members of the King family supported claims of innocence, and when Ray died in prison in Tennessee in 1998, they were invited to attend the funeral. The service was even conducted by the Reverend James Lawson, the former pastor of Centenary United who had invited Dr. King to speak to striking sanitation workers in Memphis in 1968, during which visit he was shot. Maybe they were swayed by the fact that, despite the large number of death threats directed at the civil rights leader, Memphis police quietly withdrew the expected police protection surrounding King one day before he was assassinated.

MOST MYSTERIOUS FACT

The only witness to claim he actually saw Ray at the boarding house after the shooting was Charles Stephens; other witnesses claimed that Stephens was too drunk to have seen anything. His wife refuted her husband's story, insistently claiming the man she saw in the boarding house was not Ray. The authorities went with her husband's story. For her troubles, Mrs. Stephens was committed to a mental institution.

SKEPTICALLY SPEAKING

Of all the political assassinations in the 1960s, all with disturbingly clear government ties, the murder of Martin Luther King Jr. has to vie with Robert F. Kennedy's for the title of being the most arrogant. It is staggering that it took the FBI over fifteen days to publicly announce that a bundle, thrown by the assassin, belonged to James Earl Ray. Perhaps they should have announced they were giving him a head start as well.

4 DEATH OF A DREAM— ASSASSINATION OF RFK

Around midnight on June 5, 1968, there was magic in the air at the plush Ambassador Hotel in Los Angeles. Glamorous, charismatic, and idealistic, Senator Robert F. Kennedy had just won the California primary for the Democratic nomination for president. It looked like he was going to fulfill the dreams of many Americans and go all the way to the White House—just like his brother, John F. Kennedy, had done before him.

Riding on the applause and congratulations of hotel workers, supporters, and watching members of the public, RFK was being escorted by his security team through the hotel's pantry when his charge toward the presidency came to a tragic halt in a hail of gunfire. The hopes of many Americans lay dead on the tiled floor of the pantry.

After a fierce struggle that saw a small man, seemingly possessed of superhuman strength, hold his own against several security guards, the apparent gunman—Sirhan Bashira Sirhan—was wrestled to the floor. His eyes were said to be enormously peaceful, and the suddenly tranquil assailant was arrested. At the police station, Sirhan claimed to have no memory of what had happened and showed all the symptoms of having been hypnotized.

The Los Angeles Police Department investigation into the murder quickly concluded that Sirhan was just another nut—a lone assassin in the mold of Lee Harvey Oswald. The courts agreed, and Sirhan was convicted and thrown in jail. As far as officialdom was concerned, the tragic matter was over. As for the conspiracy theorists, the shooting of RFK is a case that definitely deserves to be looked at again.

THE STRANGE PART

At first glance, the RFK case seems open and shut. There is no denying it; Sirhan was arrested with a gun in his hand at the scene. However, that is where all simplicity in this case ends. Sirhan was in the wrong position and out of range, and he could not have shot Robert Kennedy. The senator was shot from behind, but all witnesses placed Sirhan in front of him in a face-to-face position. All witnesses placed Sirhan's gun as being between one and five feet from Senator Kennedy, but the autopsy findings clearly establish that the senator was shot from a weapon held between less than one inch and no more than three inches away from his body.

THE USUAL SUSPECTS

The CIA

If, as many people suspect, the CIA had a hand in the assassination of Robert Kennedy's brother, John F. Kennedy, then they would certainly have a significant reason to fear Robert becoming president. If RFK reached the White House, he would probably launch an investigation into his brother's death—an investigation that could have proved the Warren Commission was nothing more than a cleverly constructed cover-up and that President John F. Kennedy had been removed in what amounted to a military coup.

Mafia

When his brother was president, Robert Kennedy had been attorney general and led a successful war against the Mafia. They could have decided that if RFK gained power there would be no way to prevent him from continuing his war against them even more effectively. In this situation, the traditional Mafia solution involves bullets and hit men.

Military Industrial Complex

Kennedy had pledged to end the war in Vietnam if he became president. Given the vast amounts of money that the American

RFK is shown here after winning the California primary and minutes from death.

misadventure in Southeast Asia was generating for the military industrial complex, it is certain that its members would have done anything in their power to stop his election to the White House.

THE UNUSUAL SUSPECTS

MJ-12

MJ-12, also known as Majestic 12, an ultrasecret cabal of scientists, senior members of the intelligence community, and of the military, is understood by some to be the force behind the conspiracy to suppress the truth about UFOs and aliens. Already suspected of putting an end to JFK, MJ-12 might have killed RFK to prevent him from exposing their dealings with aliens when he became president.

Neo-Nazis

Some conspiracy theorists feel that Robert Kennedy's ability to appeal both to black and to white voters would have allowed him to heal the racial divide in America and forge a nation free of discrimination and hatred. Obviously, this is not the type of place those who cherish the Nazi philosophy want to live in, so it is speculated that a cabal of neo-Nazis used their connections inside the U.S. intelligence community to carry out the execution of the enemy they feared most.

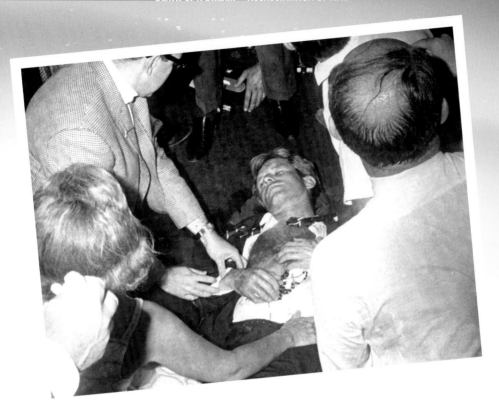

Another Kennedy is killed.

MOST CONVINCING EVIDENCE

Bullet holes in a door frame at the crime scene, which are documented in FBI photographs, clearly show that more bullets were fired than could have come from the gun Sirhan is meant to have used to kill Kennedy. The police never disclosed that these bullets existed, even though the removal of the spent bullets by LAPD investigators was witnessed by other police personnel. The door frame in question was then destroyed by order of the court directly after Sirhan's trial concluded.

MOST MYSTERIOUS FACT

According to the psychological evaluation presented in court, Sirhan was definitely under a form of hypnosis at the time of the killing. Officially, this state was described in court as self-hypnosis, but others have doubted this. Claims have been made that the late hypnosis expert William Bryan boasted that he had hypnotized Sirhan. This might not amount to much if it were not for the fact that in Sirhan's diaries, which are filled with strange writing, one name is scratched into the paper over and over: DeSalvo. It might not be a coincidence that Bryan's most famous hypnotic subject was the alleged Boston Strangler—Albert DeSalvo.

SKEPTICALLY SPEAKING

The RFK conspiracy is probably one of the hardest to be skeptical over, but it would be dangerous to underestimate what a determined lunatic can achieve when he has easy access to a powerful handgun. Especially when scandalously bad security allows that same armed lunatic to be given a perfect opportunity to shoot someone famous.

5 CHANDRA LEVY

When the skeletal remains of missing former Washington intern Chandra Levy were found in a Washington, D.C., park in May 2002, almost thirteen months after she vanished without a trace, a missing persons case became a murder investigation, and a political scandal developed into a full-blown conspiracy theory. When she came to Washington to begin an internship at the Federal Bureau of Prisons in September 2000, Levy was just twenty-two. Within weeks, friends had introduced her to Democratic congressman Gary Condit, who represented her home district in California.

Condit, a member of the U.S. Congress since 1989, was married and the father of two adult children. A major political player in Washington, he had founded a voting coalition of conservative and moderate congressmen. He also sat on several committees connected to espionage

agencies and acted as an overseer of the CIA, through his work as a member of the House Permanent Select Committee on Intelligence. Her role at the Federal Bureau of Prisons involved making access arrangements for the press to view the execution of Timothy McVeigh, the man convicted of the Oklahoma City bombing. (To many conspiracy cynics, he is known as Lee Harvey McVeigh, due to their belief that he was merely a patsy.) Levy had access to sensitive bureau and Department of Justice records relating to the condemned prisoner.

On Monday, April 23, 2001, Levy was somewhat surprisingly released from her internship. A mere week later, she was seen alive for the last time when she called in to cancel her membership at the Washington Sports Club. When her worried parents contacted the police on Saturday, May 5, 2001, they searched her apartment and found suitcases packed and ready to leave but no trace of Levy. Officially declared missing, suspicion began to build on Condit and the nature of his relationship with Levy.

Over a year later, Levy was still missing, and with his reputation in shreds, Condit was ousted from his seat in the Democratic primary by Dennis Cardoza, a former member of his own staff. However, the eventual discovery of Levy's body did not even begin to answer any of the questions her family, the police, and conspiracy theorists had as to why she had gone missing in the first place.

Chandra Levy had wanted to be a spy from an early age.

THE STRANGE PART

Levy's skeleton was found by a man walking his dog in Rock Creek Park, in an area previously searched by the police and just 300 yards (274 meters) from a running path that she was known to have used. Police discovered Levy had looked at a Web site about the Klingle Mansion, a farmhouse built in 1823 and now used as park offices, on the day she disappeared, which made the park a major focus of the investigation. Given that it was not buried, how come it took almost thirteen months to find her body?

THE USUAL SUSPECTS

The CIA

Given Condit's role in overseeing the CIA, many believe that it was something he discovered in this capacity that led to Levy's death. Her disappearance not only helped to remove him from any position of power over the agency, it also served as a warning of the fate that might lay in store for him if he shared his knowledge with anyone else.

The FBI

At the time of Levy's disappearance, questions were mounting with regard to the FBI and its investigation of Timothy McVeigh.

An affair with Chandra Levy and her subsequent disappearance cost Congressman Gary Condit his career.

A court battle over evidence that the FBI had concealed led to a delay in the planned date of his execution. Did Levy's work involving that execution lead her to discover something about McVeigh that may have made the FBI take a hand in arranging her fatal vanishing act?

THE REPUBLICAN PARTY

Even former first lady Hillary Clinton talks about a "vast right-wing conspiracy" against successful Democrat politicians. So it is no surprise that there are those who believe that the whole Chandra Levy affair was a plot by a clique of renegade Republicans to unseat Condit and, yet again, drag the Democratic political establishment through the mud.

THE UNUSUAL SUSPECTS

Mossad

Ever since she had been a little girl, Levy had wanted to be a spy, and she and other members of her family had strong connections with Israel. Some theorists believe that she had been recruited by Mossad—the Israeli secret service—to infiltrate the highest possible levels in Washington, possibly to provide future blackmail on key politicians. If agents of the United States or a country hostile to Israel had discovered this, it could certainly have been a motive for her death.

Members of Condit's Staff

Not every conspiracy needs to be about global politics. Often it can be local or personal. If that is the case with Chandra Levy, then it is easy to understand why some have already pointed the finger at members of Condit's own staff, who may have wanted to expose the congressman for either personal or Democratic Party benefit.

MOST CONVINCING EVIDENCE

Given Condit's sensitive position as a member of the House Permanent Select Committee on Intelligence and the access he had to highly classified intelligence, one of the most surprising and suspicious elements of the Chandra Levy case is just how little interest the U.S. Secret Service took in her disappearance. In most other countries, if an intern of the Federal Bureau of Prisons, who was connected to a politician with close links to foreign intelligence, disappeared, it would not just be the conspiracy theorists massing to try and find out what happened to her. The absence of serious investigation by the shadowy forces responsible for security of the state convinces many that a full-blown cover-up is involved. Conspiracy theorists believe the reason the government is not looking is because they already know the answers — they just do not want anyone else to know.

MOST MYSTERIOUS FACT

The lead FBI investigator in the Chandra Levy case was Special Agent Bradley J. Garrett, someone who had already come to the attention of some conspiracy researchers. Garrett had played a key role in the prosecution of Pakistani national Mir Aimal Kasi, who was accused of murdering CIA agents in a car parked outside the agency's headquarters in Langley, Virginia. He had also investigated the suspicious death of another young female intern—Mary Caitrin Mahoney—shot in what seemed like a professional hit in a Washington, D.C., Starbucks. Being an FBI agent involved in two conspiracies with unresolved questions makes you either incredibly unlucky or highly suspicious in the eyes of conspiracy research, but three? Not even Fox Mulder from *The X-Files* was that unlucky.

SKEPTICALLY SPEAKING

An unknown random attacker murders a young woman. Sadly, this is hardly an uncommon occurrence. Were it not related to Chandra Levy, conspiracy theorists would have their work cut out finding anything to worry about. Give it up, boys! Washington, D.C., is convoluted and murky enough without having to invent new twists and turns through the cesspool.

6 DAVID KELLY

A government scientist reveals to a journalist the truth about false evidence designed to make the public accept an unpopular war and is then found dead in suspicious circumstances. It sounds like the plot of a major Hollywood thriller. However, it happened in one of the most high-profile and intriguing conspiracies of recent times, when the British government's leading arms expert, Dr. David Kelly, was found dead in a field near his home with his left wrist slashed.

Weeks before his death, Kelly was thrust into the media spotlight after being revealed as the man the government believed could be a source for a BBC (British Broadcasting Company) report on Iraq. Although briefing journalists was part of his job, Kelly was shocked when he became a key public figure in the disagreement between the government and the BBC over claims that Downing Street had altered a dossier concerning Iraq's weapons capability.

Dr. David Kelly found himself caught in the global glare of the media.

The Oxford-educated microbiologist was the scientific adviser to the government's proliferation and arms control secretariat. Kelly was also senior adviser on biological warfare for the United Nations in Iraq between 1994 and 1999. Nominated for a Nobel Peace Prize, he was renowned for being so bright "his brain could boil water." He had been the UN weapons inspector who had previously discovered Iraq's radioactive material. He was so good at his job that Saddam Hussein was reported to have said that he should be thrown out of the country.

Kelly found himself at the center of a huge political scandal after government rules were breached, and he was exposed as the source for the BBC story that questioned Prime Minister Tony Blair's claims about weapons of mass destruction. He was forced to give evidence in public to the Foreign Affairs Select Committee on July 15, 2003. Two days later, Dr. Kelly left his home at 3 PM, telling his wife he was going for one of his regular walks. When he failed to return home by 11:45 PM, his family contacted the police.

The next morning the Thames Valley police made public his disappearance, shortly before they found a body in the woods on Harrowdown Hill, near his Oxfordshire home. As Blair struggled to answer questions about Kelly's death during a press conference in Japan, police and MI5 officers were sweeping through the germ warfare expert's house in search of "relevant documents."

Quickly reported as an apparent suicide, public specu-lation over the circumstances surrounding the death of Kelly and the media's focus on the case meant the government was forced to hold a judicial inquiry into the affair. Headed by Lord Hutton, the inquiry aimed to investigate the circumstances of his death and the allegation that the government doctored intelligence reports.

Professor Sergei Rybakov, one of Russia's top scientists and a former colleague of Kelly, immediately cast doubt on the alleged suicide. Rybakov asserted, "David was optimistic and never lost his cool even under extreme pressure. He was not capable of committing suicide."

Rybakov's claims gained weight when the inquiry found that four months before his death, Kelly had predicted that if

Harrowdown Hill, the scene of Kelly's death. Was it suicide or murder?

the American and British invasion of Iraq went ahead, he would "probably be found dead in the woods." His chilling and accurate prediction was made in February 2003 during a conversation with David Broucher, British ambassador to the disarmament conference in Geneva.

THE STRANGE PART

Aside from prophesying his own death, not leaving a note to his beloved wife, and being a member of the Baha'i faith, which is opposed to suicide, there is the question of an e-mail Dr. Kelly sent before his death. At the Hutton inquiry it emerged that he had sent an e-mail to an American journalist warning that "many dark actors are playing games" hours before he walked to the woods where he died.

THE USUAL SUSPECTS

MI6

Many parapolitical researchers believe that Kelly was murdered by security services as an example to others tempted to reveal elements of their shadowy world. Whether or not an elected official sanctioned the killing, many feel that the most likely executioners would have been MI6 personnel, especially given their links to Kelly and his work for them debriefing Russian and Iraqi defectors.

DEFENSE INTELLIGENCE AGENCY

Dr. Kelly's work with the Iraq Survey Group, set up by America and Great Britain to track down Saddam Hussein's alleged WMD arsenal, meant he came into contact with the Pentagon's Defense Intelligence Agency. Kelly had vast experience of Iraq and was one of the few people to have ever questioned Dr. Rihab Taha, the head of Hussein's biological weapons program. After the war he could have proved that the DIA's evidence to justify the war was false. With their reputation at stake, the DIA not only had a motive but are viewed by many conspiriologists as one U.S. security agency competent enough to have organized the murder.

THE UNUSUAL SUSPECTS

Iraqi Secret Service

Kelly was a thorn in the side of the Iraqi military and intelligence forces. His work had enraged Saddam Hussein and had done much to create the view in America that Iraq had never fully abandoned its WMD program. In the aftermath of the invasion, Iraqi sleeper agents may have been awakened and sent to kill Kelly in reprisal for helping bring about the invasion. If this was true, the Iraqi secret service not only got revenge against Kelly and embarrassed Blair's government, but created a suspicious climate in which their rivals in American and British secret services were thought most likely to have been involved in Kelly's death.

Unit 13

Alleged to be named after Britain's black ops death squad, formed from SAS members working for rogue elements of MI6 with strong links to the U.S. military industrial complex, Unit 13 has been accused of politically motivated assassinations and removal of "embarrassing" individuals. Infamous for a range of "death from above wet operations"—especially in Northern Ireland—it has a notorious dislike for those it regards as traitors to its country. Some of its members may have taken it upon themselves to punish Kelly for his perceived disloyalty to Blair or to protect the interests of those involved in biological warfare research.

MOST CONVINCING EVIDENCE

Michael Page, the assistant chief constable of Thames Valley Police, told the Hutton inquiry he did not think anyone else could have been involved in Kelly's death. However, this is not the view of some of his officers as expressed in off-the-record conversations with the author. Suspicions were first raised because, despite his position as a security threat, there were apparently no police, MI5, or security service observing Kelly's movements—a breach of standard protocol.

Some officers have doubts that Kelly could have slashed his wrist and then walked yards to conceal himself without leaving a trail of blood. They are worried about reports of three men dressed in black in the area where Kelly's body was found. Explained away as policemen, testimony to the Hutton inquiry by one of the officers alleged to be one of the three men clearly proves that whoever the three were, they were not Thames Valley's finest. Also troubling is that Page had to tell the inquiry how Dr. Kelly's dentist contacted the police after his death. Mysteriously, the scientist's dental records had gone missing from a locked filing cabinet on the day of his death and eventually reappeared the following Sunday.

MOST MYSTERIOUS FACT

Some conspiracy researchers feel that Kelly's death had little to do with Iraq and is actually part of a much larger conspiracy involving the deaths of at least twenty of the world's top micro- biologists within a year of each other. Many of the scientists—such as Russian defector Vladimir Pasechnik, whom Kelly had debriefed for MI6—had worked with Kelly. Among the strange deaths recorded are Benito Que (beaten in Miami); Robert M. Schwartz (stabbed in a "ritualistic slaying"); Nguyen Van Set (died in a lab freezer); and Tanya Holzmayer, killed by a microbiologist colleague, Guyang Huang, who shot her before apparently turning the gun on himself.

SKEPTICALLY SPEAKING

The Hutton inquiry failed—some might say deliberately—to answer many outstanding questions surrounding the suspicious elements of Dr. Kelly's demise. Ultimately, however, blame for the tragic death of this decent man has been laid at the door of the scientist himself. Lord Hutton found that the Ministry of Defense had not failed in its care of duty to its employee and, certainly for the foreseeable future, the case is now closed.

7 Dorothy Kilgallen

O f all the mysterious deaths that swirled around the assassination of John F. Kennedy in 1963, few are as curious as that of Dorothy Kilgallen. What separates the tragic loss of Kilgallen from the scores of officially unrelated deaths connected to that fateful day in Dallas is that Kilgallen was a popular member of the media, very much in the public eye long before her involvement in the investigation surrounding the assassination. But as her death may prove, even celebrity may not be enough to protect you if you cross the wrong people.

Kilgallen's media career began in 1931 when she signed on to work for the Hearst newspaper syndicate as a fledgling writer. At first, she was relegated to writing about "woman things," but her ambition and skill soon overrode the chauvinistic limits placed upon her, and she moved on

Kilgallen was set to expose the Warren Commission as a sham to fool the public.

to far meatier stories, including covering the legendary Sam Sheppard trial. (Sheppard's story was the basis for the popular 1960s television series *The Fugitive* and the subsequent Harrison Ford movie of the same name.) Not content with simply being a top-notch writer, Kilgallen moved into other media, working as a panelist on the popular television show *What's My Line?*, as well as hosting her own radio show in New York—a program so successful that it ran for some twenty years after first hitting the airwaves in 1945. Her popularity, buoyed by her sharp wit and intelligence, endeared her to many fans.

But it was during the trial of Jack Ruby for the murder of alleged Kennedy assassin Lee Harvey Oswald that Kilgallen may have taken the first steps that would lead to her death. After attending Ruby's murder trial in Dallas in 1964, Kilgallen became convinced that there was more to the story than was being reported in the press. After voicing her doubts in her daily newspaper column, *The Voice of Broadway*, Kilgallen returned to Dallas to interview Ruby. Excited by what she learned, she returned to New York and wrote a column that linked Dallas police officer J.D. Tippit (thought to have been shot dead by Oswald shortly after the assassination as he tried to flee) to Jack Ruby and Bernard Weissman—a man who was publicly known to dislike Kennedy. In her column, Kilgallen revealed that all three men had met in Ruby's strip club just one week before Kennedy was shot.

After she revealed more ominous material, the FBI launched an investigation into Kilgallen. But still she persevered, undeterred. She traveled to New Orleans, ostensibly to gather further proof of a cover-up, then returned home with plans to reveal all in a book. The threat that Kilgallen posed to the forces behind Kennedy's assassination may have caused her demise. Dorothy Kilgallen was found dead in her bed on November 8, 1965. The official explanation of her death was "accidental." An autopsy found an acute mix of ethanol and barbiturates in her system, so suicide could have been the cause of death. But why would Kilgallen commit suicide when the book of her career was set to be published? Was her death truly accidental? Or was she silenced, as were so many, because of her knowledge of the truth surrounding the Kennedy assassination?

THE STRANGE PART

None of the files Kilgallen had compiled, including the transcripts of her interview with Jack Ruby and the information she gleaned in New Orleans, was ever released to the media.

THE USUAL SUSPECTS

The FBI

J. Edgar Hoover himself ordered the investigation into Kilgallen, determined to discover just how she was uncovering her information, especially her publication of Ruby's testimony to the Warren Commission. Before Kilgallen broadcast that to the world, it had been classified top secret. Kilgallen's refusal to be cowed by the FBI combined with her determination to reveal the truth behind Kennedy's death—including suspected FBI involvement—may have sealed her fate.

The Mafia

Another suspect in the Kennedy assassination, the Mafia, may have silenced Kilgallen, trying to make her death look like a suicide. The Mafia may have been acting on its own or under orders from the FBI or the CIA.

Also suspected: agents of the military industrial complex; pro-Castro Cubans; anti-Castro Cubans.

THE UNUSUAL SUSPECTS

Richard Kollmar

Richard Kollmar, Kilgallen's husband, was in the apartment at the time of her death and reportedly didn't find her body until noon the next day. There are rumors that she was romantically involved with singer Johnny Ray. Allegedly, she called him from a public pay phone to say that she had the story of the century, but that she didn't feel comfortable talking about it over the phone. Her husband's jealousy as a result of this affair may have played a role in Kilgallen's demise.

Jealous Rivals

Kilgallen made no secret of the impact she felt her investigations would have. In the cut-throat world of journalism, where a single scoop can make or break a career, someone may have decided to trim the competition.

MOST CONVINCING EVIDENCE

Kilgallen was found in bed, apparently having died while reading a book. Her glasses—which she needed in order to read—were not on her face, nor within her reach. The book was one she had told friends she had already finished reading, and she was still wearing makeup, which Kilgallen always removed before going to bed.

MOST MYSTERIOUS FACT

Shortly after Kilgallen's death, Mrs. Earl T. Smith, a close friend of Kilgallen, also died mysteriously.

SKEPTICALLY SPEAKING

It's okay to report the truth—just make sure it's the approved truth.

8 THE DISAPPEARANCE OF PHILIP TAYLOR KRAMER

Rock stars who vanish or stage their own deaths are as much a part of the staple diet of conspiriologists as aliens, Masons, and the CIA. Therefore, it should not come as much of a surprise that when the former bassist of rock band Iron Butterfly joined the ranks of the missing, conspiracy theories about his disappearance would quickly start to circulate.

However, Philip Taylor Kramer was not your average rock star, and his disappearance certainly ranks as a lot more mysterious than your average conspiracy revolving around a musician who decides to "do an Elvis." For starters, as well as being a former rock musician in a successful 1970s act, Kramer was a mathematical and computer genius who had worked for the U.S. government on projects related to developing nuclear missile technology.

In the days and weeks before his disappearance on the morning of February 12, 1995, Kramer was very excited about the prospect of making a major technological break-through. Reliable sources have reported that the innovation was either in the field of fractal data compression or faster-than-light communication—two areas in which a major advance would have radically changed the face of science and commerce.

On the morning he vanished, Kramer set out in his van to pick up an associate from Los Angeles International Airport. The last person to see him was his father-in-law—a cancer patient at a medical center—with whom, it is alleged, Kramer left a small device. An unpaid airport parking charge proves that he arrived at the airport and spent forty-five minutes there, but he did not pick up the person he went to meet. Before driving into oblivion he made a series of odd phone calls to family and friends. His last call was to an emergency operator and finished with the words: "I'm going to kill myself and, I want everyone to know, O.J. Simpson is innocent, they did it."

Kramer was carrying credit cards, a bank card, and a mobile phone, none of which has been used since February 12, 1995, when he and his van pulled a perfect vanishing act. Unlike Elvis, he has never been spotted flipping burgers or serving shakes—a singular and significant fact in the disappeared-rock-star conspiracy field.

Even when his Ford Aerostar van was discovered by hikers at a Malibu ravine, on May 29, 1999, questions remained. Some doubted the skeletal remains in the vehicle belonged to Kramer, and those who were sure it was his body were more convinced than ever before that he was a victim of foul play.

THE STRANGE PART

Ron Bushy, cofounder of Iron Butterfly and a close friend of Kramer's, was one of the last people to speak to him on the day he vanished. Shortly afterward, he said, "I honestly believe that he has been abducted by our government or an agency that is part of it or maybe a foreign government or a company." The reason for this was that the mathematical breakthrough Kramer was working on could in theory have allowed for the nearly instantaneous transmission of matter. As Bushy also said, "We are talking 'Beam me up Scotty' time!"

THE USUAL SUSPECTS

The NSA

The National Security Agency has a keen interest in any development in computing that has the potential to change the nature of communications technology or affect the NSA's ability to crack codes. If Kramer had found a method of perfecting fractal compression it could have meant that even the NSA's most powerful supercomputers would not have been able to defeat the likely advance in cryptography the discovery would have offered. Faced with the possibility of unbeatable computer security, the NSA may have decided to spirit Kramer away before a foreign government did.

The Computer Corporations

If Kramer had made the breakthrough on fractal compression, it would have revolutionized the computing industry, making redundant all of the current software, and modem and chip development in which the major computer corporations have invested hundreds of billions of dollars. Faced by financial ruin, it is possible that some of the major players in this sector may have felt it necessary to prevent Kramer from revealing the nature of his breakthrough.

THE UNUSUAL SUSPECTS

Philip Taylor Kramer

All rock stars who disappear seem to be suspected of faking their own deaths, and Kramer is no exception. Some conspiracy buffs feel he disappeared to avoid financial problems, while others think it is more likely that he has gone into hiding to protect his family and to be able to work on his innovative theories without interference from the government or anyone else.

Aliens

Given that Kramer's ideas seem capable of fulfilling many of the prophecies of science fiction, it is not too surprising to find that there is a section of the conspiracy community that is convinced that little grey men, rather than human forces, spirited Kramer away. After all, they reason, if Kramer had been able to pass on the secrets of his breakthrough, their superiority in the technology stakes would have been compromised.

MOST CONVINCING EVIDENCE

James A. Traficant Jr., the representative for Ohio, has made two attempts to get the FBI to investigate the case on the grounds that the nuclear technology knowledge that Kramer possessed make his disappearance a matter of national security. Usually it does not take a politician to point out to the FBI and the intelligence services that the disappearance of a major scientist with close ties to the defense industry is worthy of investigation—especially when he designed the guidance systems for the majority of America's nuclear missiles. It is significant that the authorities' interest in Kramer's disappearance has been minimal, verging on the negligent.

MOST MYSTERIOUS FACT

In the last few days before he vanished, Kramer told his wife, Jennifer: "Honey, we are going to have to live behind walls. Honey, people are going to want to get at me." His paranoia seems to have been grounded in reality. It is reported by his father, Raymond Kramer—a fellow scientist—that their laboratory was broken into more than once, and that the intruders unsuccessfully attempted to breach the security of their computer system to gain access to data on Philip's "breakthrough."

SKEPTICALLY SPEAKING

By all accounts, in the weeks before he vanished, Kramer was a man under stress and short on sleep—two elements that may have plunged him into a state in which he could have wandered off without any memory of who he was. One or two black-hearted skeptics have commented that a man who is crazy enough to believe that O.J. Simpson is innocent is, without a doubt, sufficiently mentally troubled to attempt suicide.

9 Lord Lucan

One of the most mysterious vanishing acts ever accomplished by a fugitive was the disappearance of Richard Bingham, the seventh Earl of Lucan. "Lucky" Lucan was a member of the aristocracy and a professional gambler, a man with a well-known taste for the easy life. A popular socialite in well-to-do London circles, Lucan's expensive hobbies had left him heavily in debt. He had become estranged from his wife, and the couple were in the process of fighting a bitter custody struggle over their three children.

On the night of November 7, 1974, the twenty-nine year-old nanny who looked after Lucan's children, Sandra Rivett, was brutally murdered in the family's home with a length of lead pipe. When Lady Veronica Lucan went to investigate, she, too, was attacked and badly injured. The alarm was raised when she staggered into a pub close to the house, covered in blood, declaring that her husband had murdered the nanny.

Penniless and without his passport, that same night Lord Lucan left a letter saying that he was innocent. He borrowed a friend's car (the bloodstained vehicle was later retrieved at Newhaven Docks) and then vanished. The last sighting in the UK of the man himself had him some 18 miles (29 km) away, in the town of Uckfield. Many find it significant that although his children eventually had Lucan declared financially dead, his eldest son was not allowed to have him declared legally dead until the day after the hereditary peerage was abolished in 1999. If this had happened before, his son could have inherited his father's seat in the House of Lords.

THE STRANGE PART

Much like Elvis, Lucan is regularly sighted around the world. Reports have placed him walking on mountain slopes in Sicily and in permanent residence in southern Africa. Scotland Yard still investigates supposed sightings of the earl and has had as many as seventy different sighting reports under investigation at once. If he is still alive and in hiding, Lucan would be in his seventies, having been penniless and on the run for well over a quarter of a century.

THE USUAL SUSPECTS

Lord Lucan—Dead

The most common theory is that the earl is dead, having committed suicide in despair and remorse after bungling his attempt to kill his wife. He drove to the English coast and then swam out into the English Channel to drown.

Lord Lucan—Alive

In this version, Lucan was helped out of the county by a rich friend—possibly the now-deceased Sir James Goldsmith—who flew him from the south of England to France in a private plane. The benefactor also provided money and clothing. Once within continental Europe, it would have been relatively simple to move around without a passport—border controls are often lax—and slowly make his way down to Botswana, where he now lives. Funded by people who would rather not see the peerage dragged into disrepute by a trial, he lives in modest comfort.

THE UNUSUAL SUSPECTS

Freemasons

While it is uncertain whether or not Lucan was a Freemason, many members of the nobility are part of the ancient fraternity. Uncertain of Lucan's guilt but desperate to prevent a hugely

embarrassing trial, the Masons helped "Lucky" out of the country and set him up with a peaceful life somewhere out of the way.

Meonia

Lucan may have been a member of Meonia, a mysterious organization dedicated to preserving the bloodline of certain aristocratic British families and ensuring the continuation of Britain through mystic means. If one of their own was in trouble, the secret order would have seen it as their sacred duty to protect him from the threat of prison.

MOST CONVINCING EVIDENCE

Even though his children eventually managed to have Lucan declared legally dead, the English police were far from convinced. In interviews conducted by the author in 1999, some detectives at Scotland Yard announced a suspicion that Lucan is living in Botswana in southern Africa and that frequent trips made by his children to the area have been observed. Lack of funds made an investigation difficult to carry out. Lucan's children, however, dismissed the suggestion as absurd.

Have you seen this man? Lord Lucan is still missing.

Despite claims, the hippie known as Jungle Barry was not the seventh Earl of Lucan.

MOST MYSTERIOUS FACT

In 2003, a furor was caused when a photograph of an elderly man, claimed to be Lord Lucan, was published as part of the publicity for a book claiming that the missing earl had died in Goa, India, in 1996. However, it later turned out that the photograph of a disheveled man with a long beard bearing a resemblance to the seventh Earl of Lucan—taken in 1991—was actually that of hippie and one-time folk singer

Barry Halpin. Also known as "Mountain" or "Jungle Barry," Halpin was a heavy-drinking, banjo-playing ardent socialist who went to live in India because it was cheap, sunny, and spiritual.

SKEPTICALLY SPEAKING

As the publicity around the mistaken Halpin photo showed, Lucan has become something of a popular tragic-heroic figure. He has even adorned an album cover of English pop band Black Box Recorder and been the subject of one of their songs. Given that his theoretical backers are now dead, if Lucan revealed himself today he could make a fortune, and the publicity surrounding his case would make a trial almost impossible. If he returned and was exonerated of charges, there's little doubt he would become a genuine English folk hero. There's simply not enough scandal left to make hiding worthwhile anymore.

10 Lee Harvey Oswald

The history books tell us that on November 22, 1963, in Dallas, Texas, Lee Harvey Oswald shot and killed John F. Kennedy from a window in the Texas School Book Depository. The history books go on to recount that roughly forty-five minutes later, Oswald then shot and killed Officer J.D. Tippit of the Dallas police force and was later apprehended in a movie theater. Two days later, Oswald was himself shot by Jack Ruby, apparently outraged at the murder of the president. According to the Warren Commission, which investigated the assassination, there the story ends— the late Oswald was the lone gunman, there was no conspiracy, case closed.

However, conspiracy theories continue to swirl around the incidents of those fateful days in Dallas, suggesting that the least probable theory is that Oswald acted alone. There also remains the mystery of Oswald himself. Even the most cursory of glances at him and his alleged activities around Dallas in the days preceding the assassination are rife with inconsistencies and bizarre elements worthy of a conspiracy all on their own.

On October 26, 1957, Oswald joined the marines in San Diego, California. While he was in the marines, he became enamored of Russia and its politics. After a dishonorable discharge on September 13, 1960, he announced he was going to renounce his American citizenship and move to the USSR. He arrived in Moscow a little more than a month later. Traveling to Minsk, he married a woman named Marina, the daughter of a KGB colonel. The glorious life in Russia apparently soured, and Oswald returned to the United States with his wife in 1962. Back in the United States, Oswald drifted from one job to another and was suspected of an assassination attempt on Major General Edwin Walker on April 10, 1963, in Dallas.

His political views got him arrested in New Orleans on August 9 that same year when he was involved in a fight with angry Cubans while passing out "Fair Play for Cubans" pamphlets. A friend of his wife—a Russian exile with CIA connections—arranged for him to get an interview back in Dallas at the Texas School Book Depository. Lying about his past, Oswald was hired on October 15, 1963. The rest, as the books tell us, is history. Or is it?

THE STRANGE PART

There are conflicting reports of Oswald's activities before the Kennedy assassination. A Texas car salesman, Albert Guy Bogard, reported that Oswald took a car for a test-drive before the shooting, remarking about a large amount of money he would be getting soon—yet Oswald never had a driver's license. Another sighting has Oswald showing off at a Dallas area rifle range, expertly shooting the bull's-eyes in other patrons' targets—this, despite Oswald's inferior record as a marksman while in the marines. Maybe these "Oswalds" were actors hired by the true parties behind the assassination to ensure the real Oswald would pay for the crime.

THE USUAL SUSPECTS

The Mafia

Jack Ruby originally claimed he shot Oswald to spare Jackie Kennedy the pain of a public trial. However, plenty of evidence abounds that Ruby was a member of the Mafia. With several of the most believable conspiracy theories surrounding the assassination of JFK involving the Mafia, it probably is not coincidence that Ruby took out Oswald. Ruby killed Oswald to prevent the Mafia's role in the president's death being exposed.

Hardly anyone believes Jack Ruby acted alone when he shot Lee Harvey Oswald.

71

The FBI and the CIA

Even before Oswald left for the USSR, he was under FBI scrutiny. The reason for his dishonorable discharge from the marines—for wanting to be a Russian—was public knowledge, so the CIA would have the perfect fall guy: a lone assassin working for the dreaded Russians, which would play extremely well with the media.

THE UNUSUAL SUSPECTS

KGB

The KGB knew that if Oswald was ever brought before a court, his communist background and links to the KGB would emerge. If this happened, the Soviets would be suspected of organizing the Kennedy shooting, so they employed Ruby to ensure Oswald never went on trial.

MOST CONVINCING EVIDENCE

If Oswald had killed Kennedy for political reasons, then why did he not proudly take credit? Instead, he insisted until his death that he had been set up—hardly the actions of a fanatic. His murder by Jack Ruby—preventing the truth from ever coming to light—was far too convenient.

MOST MYSTERIOUS FACT

The CIA reportedly experimented with LSD on troops in Atsugi, Japan, as part of their mind-control tests in 1957. Oswald was serving with the marines there at the time.

SKEPTICALLY SPEAKING

Of course Oswald shot Kennedy and therefore it is not impossible that an outraged American might want to take revenge. If you listen to some of the conspiracy theories about him, you might also believe Oswald sank the *Titanic* and stole your newspaper this morning.

GLOSSARY

assassination The murder of a high-profile person, usually for political reasons.

autogiro A propellered aircraft that can move both horizontally and vertically more freely than an airplane.

Baha'i Also known as Bahai, a progressive Persian faith that seeks to form unity among all the major religions.

cabal A group of people engaged in a secret plot.

circumnavigate To travel completely around something, such as the globe.

conjecture An educated guess or presumption.

conspiracy theorist A person who contradicts the mainstream and believes in a secret plot without a reasonable amount of evidence.

convoluted Unclear; twisted.

cynic A person who usually assumes the worst in most situations.

dishonorable discharge A release from a military institution for bad behavior or poor performance.

dossier A file that contains a large amount of information about a person.

hypnotize To put into a trance.

idealist A person who unrealistically or naively believes that the best outcome will occur.

KGB The Russian State Security Committee.

MI5 The top British security organization.

military industrial complex The alliance of a government
and military industries.

patsy A person who is easily victimized.

Warren Commission An organization established in 1963
to investigate the assassination of John F. Kennedy,
which concluded that a conspiracy did not exist and that
Lee Harvey Oswald was the lone assassin.

For More Information

Amelia Earhart Birthplace Museum
223 North Terrace Street
Atchison, KS 66002
(913) 367-4217
Web site: http://www.ameliaearhartmuseum.org

Dorothy Kilgallen
Federal Bureau of Investigation
Freedom of Information Privacy Act
J. Edgar Hoover Building
935 Pennsylvania Avenue NW
Washington, DC 20535-0001
(202) 324-3000
Web site: http://foia.fbi.gov/foiaindex/dorothykilgallen.htm

The King Center
449 Auburn Avenue NE
Atlanta, GA 30312-9817
(404) 526-8900
Web site: http://www.thekingcenter.org

The Smoking Gun
600 Third Avenue
16th Floor
New York, NY 10016
(212) 692-7840
Web site: http://www.thesmokinggun.com

WEB SITES

Due to the changing nature of Internet links, Rosen Publishing has developed an online list of Web sites related to the subject of this book. This site is updated regularly. Please use this link to access the list:

http://www.rosenlinks.com/mc/mydd

For Further Reading

Branch, Taylor. *At Canaan's Edge: America in the King Years, 1965–68* (America in the King Years). New York, NY: Simon & Schuster, 2006.

Brandt, Charles. *"I Heard You Paint Houses": Frank "The Irishman" Sheeran & Closing the Case on Jimmy Hoffa.* Hanover, NH: Steerforth Press, 2005.

Bugge, Brian. *The Mystique of Conspiracy: Oswald, Castro, and the CIA.* Staten Island, NY: Provocative Ideas, 2007.

Netzley, Patricia D. *The Disappearance of Amelia Earhart* (The Mystery Library). New York, NY: Lucent Books, 2005.

Waldron, Lamar. *Ultimate Sacrifice: John and Robert Kennedy, the Plan for a Coup in Cuba, and the Murder of JFK.* New York, NY: Carrol & Graf, 2006.

Index

PHOTO CREDITS

Cover (right) p. 44 Dave Hartley/Rex Features; cover (left) p. 34 ABC News/Corbis; p. 7 Hulton-Deutsch Collection/Corbis; pp. 14, 28, 70 Library of Congress; p. 36 Ron Sachs/CNP/Corbis; pp. 42, 66 PressNet/Topham; p. 50 Bettmann/Corbis; p. 64 Charles Walker/Topham.

Designer: Tom Forget; **Editor:** Beth Bryan